THE DANGER-TO-SELF-OR-OTHERS EXCEPTION TO CONFIDENTIALITY

C. Emmanuel Ahia

University Press of America,® Inc.
Lanham · Boulder · New York · Toronto · Plymouth, UK

♾™ The paper used in this publication meets the minimum
requirements of American National Standard for Information
Sciences—Permanence of Paper for Printed Library Materials,
ANSI Z39.48-1992

Contents

Preface

Previously published as one of the American Counseling Association's (ACA) Legal Series, this title on, "The Duty-to-Warn Exception to Confidentiality" was widely cited and because of the enduring importance of the topic to clinicians, an updated edition is warranted.

A counselor's obligation to safeguard information shared in counseling has clinical, ethical, and legal implications. Trust between counselor and client is essential for effective counseling, and a counselor's vigilant protection of client confidences is vital to the development of that trust. If clients fear that the secrets they share in counseling may be revealed to others, they may terminate their counseling prematurely or hold back from full disclosure. The result may be unproductive and ineffective counseling.

Professional ethical guidelines for psychiatrists, psychologists, social workers, and professional counselors all speak to the importance of safeguarding confidential information. The ultimate penalty for the violation of these guidelines may be civil liability for invasion of privacy and/or license revocation. All states also have laws safeguarding confidential information, the violation of which may lead to civil liability and/or license revocation or suspension. In addition, the U.S. Supreme Court in *Jeffe v. Redmond* (1996) gave additional fortification to the importance of client(s) privacy, privileged communication and the confidentiality of the information exchanged between client and counselor during counseling.

However, under certain circumstance, there may be a countervailing duty to society to reveal those same confidences. That duty arises whenever the counselor comes to believe, through confidential communications, that the client or others may be endangered by the future actions of the client. In such situations, the counselor may have a duty to warn.

The purpose of this warning is to protect the client and others from the dangerous results of a client's mental instability or dysfunctionality. Clients are usually deemed to be dangerous when as a result of any mental dysfunction they become likely to harm themselves and others.

Unfortunately, it is not always easy for a counselor to know when and how to reveal confidential information under the duty-to-warn exception. State laws on the duty to warn are diverse. Some states have set forth clear standards by statute or case law as to when a duty to warn may arise. In other states the law is less clear, and in still others, there is no statutory or case law on the issue at all. The counselor's dilemma is that liability may arise not only from a failure to warn when a warning is required but also from a breach of confidentiality when there is no duty to warn.

The purpose of this book is to provide general ethical and legal guidelines and, where possible, specific information to help the practitioner make the best choice in this difficult area. It is intended for all mental health practitioners, including clinicians, students, and counselor educators.

We first briefly discuss confidentiality and privileged communication and then address the history and parameters of the duty-to-warn exception. Also included are frequently asked questions, guidelines for practice, and suggested readings. This edition contains many updates including the methods for effective warning of potential victims of client dangerousness.

I am indebted to Dan Martin, J.D., who was my co-author for the first edition and Theodore Remley, Ph.D., J.D. who was series editor for the American Counseling Association's (ACA) Legal Series. I thank my graduate assistant Peter Boccone for his manuscript formatting, organization and correspondence with the publisher.

Confidentiality and Privileged Communication

A counselor's obligation to protect counselor-client communication, to not reveal the confidences of his or her clients, has, primarily, four bases: professional ethics on confidentiality, state privilege laws, clients' right to privacy and relevant case law. Each of these is explored in this chapter.

Professional Guidelines on Confidentiality

Confidentiality is a client's legal and ethical right to prevent the disclosure of information revealed in counseling without his or her consent. It is basically an ethical right, and it is protected by the guidelines of all major mental health professional ethical codes, state counseling licensure laws, and national certifying agencies. Among these associations with guidelines generally protecting counselor-client communication are the American Counseling Association (2005), American Psychological Association (2003), National Association of Social Workers (1999), American Association for Marriage and Family Therapy (2001), National Association of Alcoholism and Drug Abuse Counselors (2008), American Mental Health Counselors Association (2010), American School Counselor Association (2004), and Association for Specialists in Group Work (2007).

Counselors must keep in mind that the ethical guidelines of these professional associations do no (like the state privilege laws discussed in the next section) have the force of law, although some states do address confidentiality in statutes on the licensure of mental health professional. Penalties for violating ethical guidelines may, however, include disciplinary actions by a professional association, a national voluntary certification agency, or a state counselor licensure board. Violations can also expose counselors to civil liability for invasion of privacy or breach of confidentiality.

An important step in properly addressing confidentiality issues, including informed consent, is to inform clients fully of all aspects of therapeutic confidentiality, including all exceptions, at the outset of treatment. Many professional associations require such disclosure in their ethical guidelines.

Counselors must also be aware that confidentiality requirements may vary according to the work setting in which the counseling is taking place. For example, school counselors are faced with unique ethical dilemmas in trying to balance the confidentiality rights of student clients with countervailing obligations to the school and to parents. There may also be legal requirements to release information about student clients that do not apply in nonschool settings. When difficult confidentiality questions arise, professional counselors in schools are advised to consult with colleagues, ethical committees of professional associations, or an attorney, as necessary. In all cases the needs of the client must remain paramount.

Other settings in which special rules may apply include prison counseling, group counseling, in-patient counseling, chemical dependency counseling (where federal guidelines may apply), and AIDS patient counseling. In each case, professional counselors must be guided by a concern for the special confidentiality needs of their clients while making certain that all legal and ethical regulations are followed. Whenever the counselor is in doubt he or she should consult professional literature and guidelines and, where possible, discuss the situation with a supervisor.

Informed consent disclosures. Counselors may ethically reveal a client's confidences with the informed consent of the client. Because confidentiality is a client's right, the client may waive that right if he or she so chooses. However, the waiver must be knowing and voluntary. Ideally the client ought to have the mental competency to do so.

Informed consent requirements are particularly important where severely disturbed clients are concerned. Although competence to grant consent is generally assumed, it may be necessary to assess competence to waive confidentiality carefully in the case of severely disturbed clients. If the counselor is not equipped to make such an assessment of competence may be necessary before confidential information is released.

There are also special informed consent requirements for minors, who are presumed to lack the capacity to make informed choices. Section B.5.a of the *ACA Code of Ethics* (ACA, 2005), provides guidance for counselors working with both minors and incompetents: "When counseling minor clients or adult clients who lack the capacity to give voluntary informed consent, counselors protect the confidentiality of information received in the counseling relationship as specified by federal and state laws, written policies, and applicable ethical standards." Thus the counselor is, in essence, empowered to decide for the client whether to waive confidentiality rights. The danger is that the counselor's judgment could be questioned at a later date by the client, or others acting on his or her behalf, who may in hindsight disagree with the counselor's decision that the release of confidential information was really in the client's best interest. Counselors are therefore advised to weigh all possible consequences carefully before releasing confidential information based upon their own assessment of what is best for the client.

Other ethical disclosures. In addition to waiver with informed consent, other circumstances in which a counselor may ethically disclose otherwise confidential information include the following:

1.   The counselor is legally compelled to make such disclosure in court. Most communications between mental health professionals and their clients are protected by state privilege laws. However, these laws do not cover all

2. mental health professionals, and further (as discussed in the next section), there are statutory exceptions that in certain circumstances require testimony concerning otherwise protected communications.
3. Confidential information may also ethically be disclosed to the counselor's supervisor, to clinical consultants, and to other professionals involved in the treatment process, providing the client has been informed in advance that such disclosures may be made.
4. Confidential information concerning clients under the age of 18 usually may be disclosed to the child's parents or guardian. However, if the child is approaching the age of majority, counselors should consult with other professionals, or with an attorney, particularly if there is any doubt about whether such disclosures violate state law or are not in the best interests of the child.
5. Confidential information may be shared in the interest of the operation of the system in special settings, such as within a penal system.

State Privilege Laws and Other Legal Requirements

In addition to complying with the professional and ethical guidelines on confidentiality of their professional associations, mental health professionals must also obey all legal mandates for the protection of client-counselor communication. These mandates include state privilege laws that exempt specific professionals from the requirement to reveal information in court about those with whom they have special relationships.

In the past, at common law the only special relationships to which the privilege of nondisclosure applied were attorney-client, priest-penitent, and husband-wife. Early in this century, the physician-patient relationship was added to the list. In recent years the psychologist-client relationship has also begun to be covered. Only in the past 30 years, however, has the protection of state privilege laws been in some states extended to other mental health professionals, such as licensed professional counselors, social workers, school counselors, marriage counselors, and rape and domestic violence counselors. Today, virtually all states recognize the psychologist-client privilege, and many afford similar protection to the privileged communications between clients and social workers, licensed professional counselors, school counselors, and marriage counselors.

Although, as previously mention, the U.S. Supreme Court in *Jaffe v. Redmond* extended this privilege to psychotherapists, it remains imperative for mental health professionals to determine whether their profession is covered by the privilege statute of the state in which they practice. In the absence of statutory protection, these professionals may be compelled to reveal confidential communications in court, despite ethical guidelines to the contrary. As was the case in *Jaffe v. Redmond*, it is recommended that mental health professionals resist such compulsions until they are total out of legal options.

Counselors however must be aware that there are statutory exceptions to all privilege laws under which professionals may be required to reveal otherwise privileged information. These exceptions cover situations in which state lawmakers have determined that other considerations outweigh the importance of the counselor-client privilege. Among the most common exceptions are the following:

1. **Risk to the health and safety of the client or others.** Many states now have specific statutory exceptions to their privilege laws covering the duty-to-warn situation. Thus in addition to being required to warn intended victims and law enforcement personnel of threats made by their clients, counselors may also be obliged under certain circumstances to testify in court concerning such threats.
2. **The intention to commit a crime.** Many states require testimony concerning confidential communication of a client's intention to commit a crime, even if the crime does not involve violence.
3. **Child abuse.** Virtually all states require mental health professionals to testify concerning their knowledge of child abuse committed by their clients, even where that knowledge was gained through confidential communications.
4. **Elder or disabled adult abuse.** All states now treat the abuse of the elderly or disabled adults in the same way as the abuse of children and require mental health professionals to testify about it, in abrogation of the counselor-client privilege.
5. **Client mental condition or state.** A counselor may be required to give testimony concerning knowledge of his or her client's mental condition in an involuntary commitment proceeding. In addition, if a client has raised the issue of his or her mental state in any legal proceeding, a counselor may be compelled to testify on that issue.

It should be noted, that in addition to requiring testimony in court concerning suspected child, elder, and disable abuse, most states now have laws requiring mental health professionals to report suspected child and elder abuse to appropriate agencies, even when the knowledge was gained through confidential communication with clients. The statutory penalty for failure to report often includes substantial fines, and even imprisonment. It might also lead to license revocation and civil actions.

Right to Privacy

Counselor-client communication is protected by the general right to privacy as well as by professional ethics and state privilege laws. Clients have a constitutionally protected right to keep their own intimate affairs private, and counselors who reveal a client's confidences may be liable for breach of the right to privacy. Mental health professionals and the general public also expect confidentiality in the counseling relationship. Confidentiality has, of course, important clinical implications in addition to being an ethical and legal issue. Clients who are confident that their secrets will not be revealed may be more open in counseling. Those considering seeking the help of a mental health professional may be more likely to do so if they are convinced that their confidences will be protected. Within the therapeutic relationship, confidentiality helps to maintain proper boundaries and roles, and to deal with the trust issues that many clients bring to counseling.

Breaches of confidentiality. The right to privacy may be breached by counselors in two ways: by disclosing the content of counselor-client communications or by disclosing client contact with the counselor. Both breaches of confidentiality are forbidden by professional, ethical, and/or legal standards.

A *content breach* is a disclosure of confidential client information to individuals with no right to that information. Such a breach of confidentiality may result in civil liability or license revocation. In the absence of an informed waiver, or one of the recognized exceptions, counselors should not disclose client confidences to anyone.

A *contact breach* is a disclosure to unauthorized third parties of the fact that a client is seeing a counselor. Even today, many people are not comfortable having it known that they are in therapy, and this fact should generally not be disclosed without the consent of the client. However, most laws do not directly address contact confidentiality, and thus a special contract between counselor and client may be needed. This contract should state that the fact the client is in therapy will not be revealed except in specifically enumerated situations. A breach of contact confidentiality is unethical and unprofessional and can lead to license suspension or civil liabilities if the breach is shown to be a proximate cause of a client's harm.

Protecting against breaches of confidentiality. Any breach of confidentiality, in the absence of a recognized exception, may lead to sanctions, including expulsion from a professional association, loss of certification, license revocation or suspension, and civil liability. Because of unauthorized disclosure of confidential information, mental health professionals have been held civilly liable for invasion of privacy, breach of confidentiality, and violation of licensing statutes.

To protect against such liability, the following steps are recommended:

1. Fully disclose, in writing, all counseling procedures and policies, including confidentiality and its exceptions, to all clients at the outset of the counseling relationship. Provide clients with complete and clear informed consent. Obtain the client's informed consent, in writing with signatures.
2. Become fully familiar with all applicable ethical and legal confidentiality guidelines, including state privilege laws and their exceptions, child, elder, and disabled abuse reporting requirements, and the parameters of the duty-to-warn exception in your state.

Confidentiality and Informed Consent

Informed Consent is a client's right to voluntarily agree to participate in counseling, clinical assessment or other mental health services *after* such services have been fully described and explained to the client in a manner that is comprehensible to the client. (Ahia, 2009) It is derived from a client's right to autonomy, privacy and self determination and is required by the code of ethics of all mental health professions. Because it is intended to ensure that a client knows the risks, benefits, and alternatives to a proposed procedure, it should be implemented preferably with a consent document that the client and counselor must sign. Should there arise a need to substantially change the treatment direction and protocols, an addendum should be added to the original consent.

The best professional practice is the use of an Informed Consent form which expressly contains conditions under which a counselor will breach confidentiality. These conditions should at the very least include legal, ethical, and professional requirements that the counselor should report child abuse, elder abuse, dangerous clients, HIPPA issues, etc. Form documentation attesting to her client's understanding and agreement to informed consent disclosures, was the reason why defendant therapist Ann Walker prevailed in a case brought against her for breach of confidentiality by client Karen McFadden. (McFadden v. U.S. Department of the Army, No. Civ. 1:03CV2237) Even if the law is clear, consent form documentation and discussion of the conditions with a client reinforce the counselor's respect and commitment to a client's dignity, autonomy and self determination.

Information Source of Client's Danger

To determine a client's dangerousness, mental health professionals typically look at the totality of a client's intrapersonal and interpersonal factors. A client's mental health diagnosis and condition, social stressors and conditions, and violence history and propensities are usually taken into account. The following sources or pieces of the puzzle should be looked into to determine a client's dangerous status for breach of confidentiality purposes:

1. Clients History
   a. A client's history of family or social violence. Persons who have in the past used violence to resolve personal issues, been repeatedly

      b.   exposed to violence or who admire the use of violence or have impulse control problems.

      c.   A client's criminal history, especially involving the use of weapons, antisocial behaviors, frequently under the influence of drugs or alcohol, or involved with gangs or hate groups.

      d.   A history of mental instability or psychosis.

2.   Present Conditions

      a.   A client who is involved in a social conflict or is angry.

      b.   A client who threatens to do harm to an identifiable person, persons, or property (depending on the state law).

             ■ When a client threatens to harm any person, even if that person knows, it is prudent to warn or "re-warn" the potential victim then not to. This should be taken seriously even if the client has no history of violence. Violent behavior starts somewhere at sometime.

3.   Reliable Informants

      a.   When other individuals inform a counselor of our client's violent intentions with reasonable specificity.

      b.   When family members of a potentially violent client inform us of our client's violent intention with reasonable specificity. In Ewing v. Goldsting (2004), the therapist was held liable for failure to breach confidentiality and warn a victim. The court considered the client's father a reliable informant of the client's dangerousness. The court implied in this case that the credibility of the source of the information is equally important.

The Duty-to-Warn Exception

In *Tarasoff v. Regents of the University of California* (1976), the California Supreme Court held that whenever a mental health professional determines, or according to the standards of his or her profession should determine, that a client presents a serious danger of violence to another, that professional has an obligation to use reasonable care to protect the client's intended victim. The *Tarasoff* court further held that the care required to protect the victim depends upon the specific circumstances of the case, and may include warning the victim, notifying the police, or taking other steps.

In *Tarasoff*, a young woman was killed by a patient who was under treatment by a licensed psychologist at the University of California at Berkeley. Ms. Tarasoff's parents brought a wrongful death action against the psychologist and the school based on the theory that because the psychologist knew that his patient was both dangerous and obsessed by Ms. Tarasoff, he had a duty to warn the potential victim of the danger. The court ruled in the parents' favor, despite the fact that the psychologist had informed the police prior to the murder.

Traditional American common law recognizes no legal duty to prevent one person from harming another, even where such help could be given without any danger to the helper. This rule has been heavily criticized over the years, and many other countries have rejected it. But with the exception of the State of Vermont, which has passed a Good Samaritan statute, it remains the law in this country: There is no general duty to help others by warning them of impending peril.

Courts have, however, carved out an exception to the nonhelp rule where a special relationship exists between the person who is aware of impending danger and the potentially dangerous person. One such special relationship, recognized by many courts, is that between a mental health professional and his or her client.

The *Tarasoff* case revolutionized duty-to-warn law for mental health professionals in this country. Prior to *Tarasoff*, a few cases had suggested such a duty, but they received little publicity and had minimal precedential impact on courts in other jurisdictions. Since *Tarasoff*, duty-to-warn cases have proliferated, and legislation has been passed in many states codifying the duty to warn.

Unfortunately for the practitioner, courts and legislatures throughout the country have been unable to agree as to the proper scope of the duty to warn. There is no one universally accepted rule, and it is therefore vital for all mental health professionals to familiarize themselves with the specific duty-to-warn rule in their own state.

Circumstances Giving Rise to a Duty to Warn

Though state laws as to the circumstances that give rise to a duty to warn do vary widely, the guidelines of all major professional associations are quite consistent. Unfortunately, these guidelines are not specific enough to be of much help to counselors faced with a difficult duty-to-warn situation. For example, Section B.2.a of the *ACA Code of Ethics* (ACA, 2005) requires counselors to ". . . protect clients or identified others from serious and foreseeable harm. . . ."

Such guidelines do provide a general basis for the ethical disclosure of confidential information to protect third parties. However, mental health professionals must look further, to specific statutes and case law in the state in which they practice, to determine whether to disclose information in particular cases.

As of writing, the issue of the scope of the duty to warn has been specifically addressed, by statute or case law, in most states. In all states where the issue has been addressed, the legislature, or the courts, has determined that there is a duty to warn third parties under certain circumstances. However, there is no consensus among the states as to the particular circumstances that may trigger the duty to warn.

The one state that at one point apparently rejected any legal duty to warn third parties is Maryland. In *Shaw v. Glickman* (1980), the Court of Special Appeals of Maryland held that because there is no exception to the state privilege law for threats to third parties, it would be a violation of the law for a psychiatrist to disclose information about dangers posed by his or her client to a potential victim. Counselors in Maryland must be careful in applying the holding of the *Shaw* case, however, because neither of the two key factors in duty-to-warn cases, a *communicated threat* against a *readily identifiable victim*, was present.

The Communicated Threat Requirement

The single most controversial duty-to-warn issue is whether a client must actually communicate to a counselor his or her intention to harm someone in order to trigger a duty to warn.

Some states (California, Colorado, Kentucky, Louisiana, Minnesota, Montana, and New Hampshire) now have statutes requiring that an actual threat be communicated in order to trigger a duty to warn third parties.

The California statute, specifically passed to limit counselor liability in the aftermath of *Tarasoff*, limits the duty to warn to situations ". . . where the patient has communicated to the psycho-therapist a serious threat of physical violence against a reasonably identifiable victim or victims" (California Civil Code, 1992, Cumulative Pocket Part 43.92(a)).

The rationale for the communicated threat requirement is the feeling that there must be an objective basis to believe that a third party is actually in danger before a counselor should be required to take the extraordinary step of breaching a confidential relationship with his or her client and warning a third party.

Other states, Alabama, Illinois, Iowa, and Pennsylvania for example, have adopted the communicated threat requirement in court decisions dealing with the issue. The requirement of a communicated threat makes the counselor's decision on whether to warn a third party much easier. A duty to warn, in states with a communicated threat requirement, is only triggered by objective, verifiable conduct on the client's part. Thus the guesswork is removed, and counselors can be fairly certain when they *must* warn third parties and when they *may not*. This, of course, does not mean that a counselor with a dangerous, decompensating client, who has not communicated a specific threat, need take no action to protect the public. When a client is seriously disturbed, and therefore a danger to him- or herself and the community, counselors still must exercise their professional judgment and take immediate steps to have the client detained and controlled until he or she is no longer dangerous. However, in states requiring a communicated threat, the counselor's responsibility ends there and does not require that additional steps be taken to warn potential victims.

The situation is quite different for counselors in states not requiring a communicated threat to trigger a duty to warn. At least four states (Massachusetts, New Jersey, Oklahoma, and Rhode Island) have adopted this position by statute. In Massachusetts, for example, a duty to warn may arise not only following a communicated threat but also if the patient ". . . had a *history of physical violence* [italics added] to believe that there is a clear and present danger that the patient will attempt to kill or inflict serious bodily injury against a reasonably identified victim. . . ." (Massachusetts General Laws, 1992b, Sec. 36B).

Here the professional is faced with the monumental task of first looking to the past to determine whether his or her client has evidenced a sufficient history of violent behavior and then deciding whether there is a reasonable basis to believe that the client is now on the verge of a violent outburst directed at a reasonably identified victim. The historical task alone is difficult enough. Is one instance of past violent behavior enough? Must the past violence have been directed at a similarly situated victim, such as a former girl friend, in order to trigger a duty to warn a current girl friend? The second determination, whether there is a reasonable basis to believe that the client is *now* about to attack a certain person in the absence of an explicit threat directed at that person, appears to be even more difficult. But though these issues may not be easy ones, they must be addressed by counselors in Massachusetts and other states that do not require a communicated threat to trigger a duty to warn.

Some other states like Alaska, Arizona, Delaware, Michigan, Vermont, Washington, and Wisconsin have adopted the Massachusetts position in recent court decisions. Professional counselors in these states must be ever on the alert for situations in which third persons may be in peril from the actions of their violent clients, whether or not actual threats have been made.

The Identifiable Victim Requirement

A second duty-to-warn issue, which has also divided courts and legislatures, is the question of how sure a counselor must be of the identity of an endangered third party before being required to warn him or her of impending peril. Clearly, a counselor must have some way of identifying the intended victim. Otherwise, he or she could not possibly warn the victim without warning every single person in the community. There are, of course, situations in which a client is so violent and out of control that there is a risk to anyone with whom he or she comes into contact. In such cases, all prudent mental health professionals will immediately notify the police and take steps to have the client detained, and perhaps involuntarily committed on an emergency basis.

When such a client is not yet in custody, counselors in states that do not require explicitly communicated threats to trigger a duty to warn are also safe in warning all those with whom the counselor expects the client to come into immediate contact — such as housemates or co-workers — if the client is headed home or to his or her job site.

A far more difficult case arises when a client is not dangerous to the whole community but may pose a real danger to one specific person or group of persons. The issue then is how to identify potential victims.

Most states require that the potential victim be identifiable in some way in order to trigger a duty to warn that specific person. But there are more important differences with respect to how specifically the potential victim must be identified. Most states with duty-to-warn statutes only require that the victim be *reasonably identifiable*. California, New Hampshire, Kentucky, Montana, Massachusetts, and Oklahoma have adopted this standard. Minnesota, Louisiana, and New Jersey require that the victim be *clearly* or *readily identifiable*; Colorado requires a warning only when a *specific* person has been threatened.

In general, most states that require a dangerousness-based-breach of confidentiality also tend to limit the duty to warn to specifically identified victims. This makes sense because victim identification is generally easier when a specific threat, and not merely a reasonable belief on the counselor's part, triggers the duty-to-warn.

Victim Identifiability Guideline.

The following may help mental health professionals in deciding who an identifiable victim may be. A potential victim may be identifiable if:

1. The dangerous client names a specific person as an object of their reasonable or unreasonable anger, grievance, or grudge.
2. The objective circumstances or facts point to a particular person or persons.

3. A credible source informs the mental health professionals that his/her client has an imminent plan to harm the victim and this information is corroborated by some of the clinical information or concerns the counselor already has about the client.
4. If clients' clearly dangerous propensities and impulses can be predictably unleashed at identifiable victims in "close-circuit" environments e.g. neighborhoods, classrooms, churches, work places, prisons, etc.

In most cases it is quite clear who must be warned, regardless of the specific identifiability language of a state's statute or case law. However, in certain cases the decision as to whether a particular person must be warned may be a difficult one. For example, in *Thompson v. County of Alameda* (1980) a juvenile offender being held in custody threatened to kill a "young child." Within 24 hours of his release, he murdered a 5-year-old neighbor. The court dismissed the parents' suit on the basis that the threat was too general to trigger a duty to warn because it would have been impractical and ineffective to warn all young children in the neighborhood.

In contrast, a California court 10 years later held in *Barry v. Turek* (1990) that a female sexual assault victim, who worked on the same floor in a psychiatric hospital as the patient who raped her, was a reasonably identifiable victim who should have been warned because the rapist had threatened and attempted to molest other females sexually on that same floor in the past.

It is clear that there is no magic formula for determining who is a reasonably identifiable victim who must be warned of the dangerous propensities of a client. In borderline situations, counselors are well advised to seek the assistance of a supervisor or an attorney because they may be subject to liability for failure to warn those entitled to warnings — or for warning those not so entitled.

The Concept of Dangerousness

One exception to the rule that counselor-client communications must be kept confidential is, as already noted, when the client is dangerous. However, before applying this exception, a determination must be made that the client is indeed dangerous as a matter of fact and law. Thus a counselor's definition of *dangerousness* must meet legal and professional standards.

In general, a dangerous client is defined as *one whose current mental condition and propensity for violence promises to lead to serious physical harm to self or others*. In determining the dangerousness of a client in the confidentiality context, a professional should attempt to answer three important questions:

1. What level of danger must be reached before confidentiality may be breached?
2. What are the legal guidelines for determining dangerousness?
3. What are the problems inherent in predicting dangerousness based upon professional standards?

Level of Danger

The level of dangerousness required before confidentiality may be breached must go beyond probability and approach certainty of danger. Mental health professionals may not breach confidentiality when they merely *suspect* or *think* a client is dangerous but only when that client is *predictably* or *certainly* harmful to self or others. Therefore there may be many potentially dangerous clients who are not dangerous enough to allow for a breach of confidentiality.

The ability to distinguish between a client who is only *potentially dangerous* and one who is *predictably dangerous* is important because civil liability could arise from a failure to predict or diagnose a client who is certainly or predictably dangerous, as in *Tarasoff*-type cases, or from incorrectly diagnosing a client as predictably dangerous when in fact he or she is not. Schutz (1982) suggested several different causes of action that could be brought by either a patient or a victim should a counselor fail to distinguish between an actually dangerous and a potentially dangerous client. A client diagnosed by a professional as posing a serious danger to self and others, but who in fact does not, could file suit for negligent diagnosis, defamation of character, or invasion of privacy if the counselor breached confidentiality and notified potential victims. Moreover, the alarmed victim could also bring action for negligent diagnosis and negligent infliction of emotional distress.

Legal Guidelines

Tarasoff, and cases following it from many jurisdictions, have left us with certain legal concepts that are helpful in determining the level of dangerousness required before a client's right to privacy may be compromised: imminent danger, foreseeable danger, danger to an identifiable victim, and existing danger. Depending on the facts of the case, any one of these concepts (or a combination of several) should help a prudent professional decide when a potentially dangerous client has crossed the line and become predictably and imminently dangerous. It is at this point that the client's right to privacy should give way to the counselor's duty to protect likely victims.

Imminent (immediate) danger. In order for confidentiality to be breached because of a client's dangerousness, a prudent professional looking at the facts presented by the mental dysfunctionality of a client must be able to predict that the client is likely to behave dangerously in the *very near future.* To decide if a client is imminently dangerous, it is necessary to look at the danger from the perspective of the time and distance it will take to accomplish the potential harm. If it is reasonable to assume that it will take little time and a short distance to accomplish the harm, the danger should be considered imminent.

Foreseeable danger. A prudent professional must be able to perceive the *unavoidability* of the danger. Here the danger is considered from the perspective of a client's *present* potential to commit harm, his or her propensity to do so, whether a plan exists, and his or her past behavior relative to the potential harm. A client who possesses the ability, has the plan, is leaning toward accomplishing the harm, and has a history consistent with such violent behavior should be considered foreseeably dangerous.

The concept of foreseeability implies that a professional's training, knowledge, and experience should enable him or her to accurately predict his or her client's violent behavior. That is the expectation of the law, although mental health professionals have expressed doubt as to whether they can in fact make such accurate predictions of violence (Cocozza & Steadman, 1975–1976).

Danger to an identifiable victim. One factor considered crucial in determining dangerousness is whether the target or object of the potential harm can be accurately and definitively identified. Can the prudent professional easily identify or specify the person(s) who are likely to be harmed by the potentially dangerous client? The existence of clearly identifiable victim(s) should help professionals in predicting whether a potentially dangerous client has become predictably dangerous. In some cases the entire public may in fact be identifiably victims.

Existing danger. This concept refers to the reality of the danger relative to the background and personality of the client. The question here is whether the prudent professional looking at the present dysfunctionality of a client in light of the client's past behavior and mental history should see that client as ready to explode at any time. Given the right time and circumstances, is this historically (potentially) dangerous client *now* likely to cause harm to self or others? In making this determination, it is helpful to look at the social circumstances of the client to see if he or she has in fact been provoked or abuse or, in the absence of actual provocation or abuse, if the client perceives him or herself as provoked or abused.

Problem in Predicting Dangerousness

Despite the legal guidelines, predicting violence remains difficult for many mental health professionals. This is in part because there are no available psychological instruments that can accurately predict violent behavior. Moreover, the formal training and orientation of mental health professionals is so diverse that a uniform diagnosis of dangerousness is difficult to arrive at in any given situation.

Whether we are counselors, psychiatrists, psychologists, or social workers, we need to become more aware of how our theoretical orientation — Adlerian, Gestalt, psychodynamic, behavioral, transactional analysis, client-centered — has an impact on our ability to predict our clients' dangerousness. While a strongly psychodynamically oriented therapist may look mainly at a client's intrapsychic profiles to determine dangerousness, an Adlerian counselor may focus more on interpersonal factors. Obviously, neither is entirely right or entirely wrong. However, a holistic approach that focuses on the past as well as the present, and on the totality of a client's behavioral, affective, cognitive, interpersonal, and social realities, may result in the most accurate and prudent professional assessment of dangerousness. To this end, it is useful to consider the following three-item conceptual checklist to ensure that no diagnostic stone is left unturned:

1. **The history of a client's violent behavior.** Assessment of a client's propensity for violence should involve a direct interview with the client and the acquisition of past mental health records. It should include an assessment not only of past actions but also of any past and present expressions of intent to commit violent acts.
2. **A client's social conditions.** Certain social conditions and circumstances are more likely than others to degenerate into violence, for example, frequent marital disagreements and the availability of a handgun in the household. It is therefore important to assess how violence prone the client's social situation really is.
3. **A client's psychological conditions.** Although no single psychological instrument can conclusively predict violent behavior, it is prudent to use whatever is available to assess a particular client's propensity for violence. Such characteristics as impulsivity and self-control, patterns of anger expression, socialization, and early childhood scripting may be helpful in determining if the client has a relatively high predisposition to violence. Schutz (1982) suggested that any client showing evidence of physiological

impairment, such as a recent head injury, should be medically examined to determine the potential for neurologically based violent behavior.

Methods for Effective Warning of Dangerousness

Once a mental health professional has made the usually painful determination that a client is a danger to self or others, it becomes important that an effective communication method be chosen in order to avert the danger. The method employed by the therapist to communicate this danger has to be that which a reasonably prudent professional will use under these particular circumstances and not any other that may have been useful in a factually different circumstance. In Emerick v. Philadelphia Center for Human Development, Inc (1998) the defendant therapist was sued for ineffective communication of the danger his client posed. The court ruled that the method the therapist chose to communicate the danger was sufficient given the circumstances.

The following methods should be considered by counselors who must effectively communicate the danger posed by their clients. Depending on the facts of a particular case, counselors may find it most prudent to use a combination of these methods.

Verbal Communication. This can be used when the client is still in the office or immediately after he or she leaves. Typically the therapist contacts the identifiable victim by phone. If the identifiable victim is unavailable, significant adults in the victim's or client's life should be contacted or the police if none of these are available. Ideally more than one attempt should be made to contact any identifiable victim or significant persons. This method implies that counselors should search for and use mobile phones when possible. This also includes 911 calls notifying law enforcement of the danger.

Written Correspondence. Sending a certified letter to the last known address of a potential victim can be overnighted if other contact information is unavailable. If the danger is very imminent, attempts should be made through the white pages or other means to locate the potential victim. This method is not the best in most cases.

Electronic Correspondences. Text messaging, emails, Facebook etc. constitute speedy means of communicating the danger posed by a client to a potential victim. However, they are not without legal and ethical pitfalls. There is typically no legal presumption that once sent the intended recipient of e-communications has received the message. Although a message may have been effectively sent it may still be residing in the phone or computer unreviewed and therefore has not been effectively received until the recipient actually opens the mail.

It is professionally important for a mental health professional to frequently review his or her electronic devices if he/she has given clients the impression that these are reliable means of quick contact with the therapist. Clients on the other hand do not have such obligation therefore electronic devices are imperfect methods for communicating a client's dangerousness. Therapists, who wish to rely heavily on electronic devices for clinical communication must for legal and ethical reasons, include this in informed consent.

In addition, therapists who rely on electronic devices must be careful not to use unstandardized wordings (e.g. "U" for "you"), confusing formatting, or misspellings. Electronic messages intended to communicate a client's dangerousness should be clear, well thought out, and legible.

A copy of all such electronic communication should be preserved for forensic reasons. Because most electronic communications are vulnerable to forgeries and can be altered, it is prudent practice and herein advised that practitioners create an archive for e-communication should there arise a need to invalidate false claims.

One very serious danger of electronic communication is that with the click of a mouse, a message can be sent to many unintended recipients. Many have in fact experienced this disaster which no mental health professional can afford when communicating that his or her named client is a danger to self or others. There is no doubt such a mistake will carry legal and ethical consequences. The following guidelines may be helpful:

1. Preserve all dangerousness e-communication for at least 7 years or in accordance with state law. This is important because the actions of a dangerous client can easily lead to litigations during which time all communications may become forensic. Destruction of such records may create suspicion of destruction of evidence.
2. Create a dangerousness e-communication archive that is protected and secure. This will help preserve authenticity in case of forgery. Encrypt when possible.
3. Before you click the send icon, make sure, absolutely sure, that you have the correct intended recipient(s) on your list.
4. The content of records that are stored in alterable forms can typically be challenged in court on the basis of accuracy. Therefore a secure storage is advised.
5. If a part of an e-communication is later found to have been illegally altered, it becomes very difficult to prove that other associated documents are unaltered. An ideal archive will allow for necessary updates and corrections in a way that will not compromise the integrity of the records

Multiple Methods. In the highly mobile world that we now live in, one method of dangerousness communication may not satisfy the typically very urgent need to contact a potential victim, victims or persons who can help avert the danger. Therefore, the use of multiple methods may be most effective and prudent and therefore highly recommended.

The Golden Rule. Effective communication of a client's dangerousness that in fact protects potential victims and property is the supreme goal of "the danger-to-self-or-others exception to confidentiality." Yet practicing professionals must keep in mind:

1. The amount of clinical information revealed by the counselor must not exceed what is necessary for the recipient to prevent the harm.
2. The recipient must be the person against whom the harm is intended or a person who is qualified or has the experience or duty to prevent the harm.

Danger to Others: An Overview

Whenever a counselor makes the difficult decision that a client is indeed dangerous to self or others, and that the duty-to-warn exception to confidentiality must be applied, the counselor must be aware of who must be warned and what the content of the warning should be. The counselor must also consider involuntary commitment for a dangerous client.

Who Must Be Warned

Although determining who to warn in a particular case is not always easy, four classes of individuals or agencies *may*, in fact, require warnings under certain circumstances:

1. **The police.** Whenever a client diagnosed as imminently dangerous to others remains at large, the prudent counselor should enlist the aid of local law enforcement authorities in having the client detained on an emergency basis. There is no risk of liability for breach of confidentiality as long as proper statutory procedures are followed and the counselor does not disclose more of the client's file than is necessary to safeguard the public.
2. **Appropriate authorities under the state's involuntary commitment statute.** In many duty-to-warn cases, the client meets statutory criteria for involuntary commitment. The counselor should be familiar with these criteria and should consider instituting involuntary commitment proceedings whenever there is a determination of dangerousness.
3. **Identifiable victims.** Whenever a counselor can be fairly certain of the intended victims of a dangerous client, those individuals should be warned immediately. The warning, however, should be limited to information necessary for the protection of the intended victim, including the identity and description of the client, and the time and place of the expected attack.
4. **Other potential victims.** Depending upon the jurisdiction, there may be a duty to warn person other than clearly identifiable victims. Counselors in states that have adopted broad duty-to-warn rules must make a considered professional judgment as to who is likely to be harmed if the client behaves in a foreseeable dangerous manner. No court, however, expects a counselor to be able to predict the behavior of a client with complete certainty. If the counselor uses reasonable care in predicting the foreseeable victims of his

or her dangerous client, and warns all such foreseeable victims, he or she will probably not be held liable if an unlikely victim is harmed.

Content of the Warning

The content of the warning depends upon the facts of the particular case and the identity of those being warned. Law enforcement personnel need to know the whereabouts of the dangerous client, including his or her address, place of employment, and other places he or she is likely to be found. They also need a good physical description of the client and as much information as possible as to the nature of the threat and the means by which the counselor expects it to be carried out. A concise explanation of the nature of the client's mental disease and current condition is also helpful to police in avoiding a violent outcome.

Information disclosed in the context of a petition for involuntary commitment is somewhat different. The emphasis here is on evidence of the current mental condition of the client, particularly with respect to his or her likelihood to harm self or others. Specific descriptions of recent actions or threats by the client that suggest imminent dangerousness should also be included.

Warnings to potential victims must provide sufficient information to avoid the danger while refraining from the disclosure of sensitive information (such as the client's diagnosis), which may not be of any help to the victim.

The Involuntary Commitment Option

The option of involuntary commitment must always be considered when a client makes threats or exhibits violent behavior. A finding of dangerousness generally forms the basis for involuntary commitment. It is always preferable for a client who requires hospitalization to be convinced to check in voluntarily. Voluntary commitment helps preserve the integrity of the counselor-client relationship because the involuntarily committed client may feel betrayed by the counselor who instituted the commitment proceedings.

If a dangerous client refuses to commit him or herself, however, the counselor must institute commitment proceedings without delay. Counselors face a grave risk of liability to anyone harmed by a client who should have been committed but was not because of the counselor's failure to take steps to commit the dangerous client. The involuntary commitment option should, of course, always be fully explained to all clients at the outset of treatment.

Danger to Others: Specific Groups

Specific duty-to-warn issues arise when clients are determines to be dangerous to self or others because they are HIV positive; because they are discovered to be child abusers, or elder or disabled adult abusers; because of spousal abuse; or because their medication, addiction, or mental disease makes them unsafe drivers.

HIV-Positive Clients

Unique duty-to-warn issues are raised when a counselor becomes aware that a client is HIV positive. All states now have statutes that specifically address the HIV situation. These statutes require that information on HIV status be kept confidential, with certain enumerated exceptions. In most states, only physicians are permitted to disclose an individual's HIV status to a patient's spouse or other known sex partners, and to those with whom the patient is known to share needles. These specific statutory provisions usually apply only to medical doctors, but counselors may have a duty to warn endangered third parties under the general duty-to-warn guidelines already discussed.

Such a duty to warn may arise when a counselor has reason to believe that his or her HIV-positive client intends to continue to have unprotected sec, or to share needles, with unsuspecting but reasonably identifiable third parties. Whether there is a duty to warn under such circumstances depends in part upon whether the counselor's state requires a communicated threat and a specifically identifiable victim.

A prudent counselor should take a number of steps with respect to the HIV duty-to-warn situations:

1. Make sure to disclose all confidentiality limits at the outset of treatment. Be aware of the latest medical information with respect to the transmission of the AIDS virus, know which sexual practices are safe and which are not, and encourage clients, regardless of their HIV status, to practice safe sex.
2. Counselors dealing with this issue must act in ways that are consistent with state HIV-Confidentiality Laws. There are three types of these laws:
    1) HIV-Specific Confidentiality Laws
        - These are laws/statutes that forbid professionals from disclosing their clients' HIV status.
    2) HIV-Partner Notification Laws

- These are laws that are exceptions to the HIV-Specific Confidentiality Laws. They authorize a healthcare professional/officer to notify the sexual or needle sharing partners of their HIV-positive client.

3) HIV-Criminal Laws
- These are statutes that criminalize sexual relationships with anyone by someone who knows that he/she is HIV positive.

3. Stress to HIV-positive clients the importance of disclosing their status to sex partners and others who may be at risk and provide clear, understandable information on safe sex immediately upon discovering the client's HIV-positive status.

4. Before disclosing the client's HIV status to sex partners or others, advise the client of the intention to do so, and of the specific actions planned.

5. In disclosing HIV information, be careful to follow the statutory guidelines and to safeguard the client's confidentiality the fullest extent possible.

The HIV-positive duty-to-warn situation is especially difficult for the counselor because he or she is faced not only with general ethical and legal confidentiality requirements for counselor-client communications but also with specific statutory prohibitions against disclosure of HIV information. However, given the sometimes clear danger of death presented by HIV transmission, the counselor should notify all potential victims of a client who is HIV-positive and who has expressed an intention to take actions that may endanger the lives of others.

Child Abusers

In virtually every state, counselors have a *statutory duty* to report information they receive about the abuse of children to the police or to a local child services agency. Minnesota's statute is typical:

> (a). . . A person who knows or has reason to believe a child *is being neglected or physically or sexually abused . . . or has been neglected or physically or sexually abuse within the preceding 3 years* [italics added], shall immediately report the information to the local welfare agency, police department, or the county sheriff if the person is:
> (1) a professional or professional's delegate who is engaged *in the practice of the health arts . . . psychological or psychiatric treatment* [italics added], child care, education, or law enforcement. . . . (Minnesota Statutes Annotated, 626.557, 1989)

It is well worth noting that, in contrast to the typical duty-to-warn situation discussed in pervious chapters, even past instances of child abuse must be reported in Minnesota and elsewhere. Most child abuse reporting statutes have four key provisions:

1. Reporting is mandatory for mental health professionals.
2. Those who do make reports are granted statutory immunity from all civil or criminal liability that might otherwise arise as a result of the report.
3. There is a statutory exception to the counselor-client privilege. Thus counselors may be required to testify in court concerning the alleged child abuse if civil or criminal litigation results from the report.
4. Severe penalties, up to and including fines of up to $1000 and imprisonment for up to a year, may result from a failure to report known or suspected cases of child abuse.

Elder and Disabled Adult Abusers

In recent years, many states have passed laws requiring mental health professional to report known or suspected incidents of the abuse of aged or disabled adults. In most cases, these statutes are very similar to child abuse reporting statutes. Once again reporting is generally (though not always) mandatory, those who report are immune from liability, the counselor-client privilege does not apply, and there are stiff penalties for failure to report. The rationale for these laws is that aged and disabled adults, like children, may not be in a position to report abuse themselves. Because not all states have such laws, and because some such laws *permit*, but do not *require*, mental health professionals to report elder and disabled abuse, all professionals are advised to check their own state's statute before reporting this type of abuse.

Spousal Abuse

Spousal abuse is a very serious problem in this country today. However, there is no recognized exception to confidentiality that permits counselors to report *past* cases of spousal abuse, unless the abuse victim is a child or an aged or disabled adult. Of course, in cases where the client has threatened to harm his or her spouse in the *future*, there may be a duty to warn if the requirements set forth in previous chapters are met.

Unsafe Drivers

One special duty-to-warn situation arises when a counselor knows, or should know, that a client is operating a motor vehicle in a dangerous manner. The client may be an alcoholic or drug addict who is under the influence when he or she arrives for counseling. The client may be taking medication that makes driving dangerous, yet he or she continues to drive to and from counseling sessions; or the client may be suffering from a mental disease that in the counselor's professional opinion makes driving unsafe.

In each of these situations, the counselor must consider taking steps to protect the public from imminent danger. In certain cases, the involuntary commitment option must be considered. For example, if a schizophrenic client either is not being helped by his medication or has stopped taking it and is losing touch with reality, it may be appropriate for a counselor to seek emergency commitment before the client injures self or others by unsafely operating a motor vehicle. Similarly, if a client is known to be driving under the influence, a counselor does not risk liability for breach of confidentiality if local law enforcement personnel are alerted to be on the lookout for the client. In these cases the safety of the public is paramount, and confidentiality must be breached.

The more difficult determination is whether to warn specific private individuals of a client's unsafe driving and, if so, who to warn. In those states that require a communicated threat, there clearly is no duty to warn any third parties. But in states that do not require such a threat, a duty may arise to warn reasonably identifiable third parties who are likely to be endangered by the client's reckless driving.

In *Schuster v. Altenberg* (1988), the husband and daughter of a psychotic woman sued her psychiatrist for injuries they suffered while passengers in her car. They alleged that the psychiatrist had a duty to warn them of the dangers of being in a car driven by the woman because he knew she was incapable of driving a car safely, given her mental condition.

The court refused to dismiss the case, rejecting the psychiatrist's argument that because the family members were not readily identifiable victims he had no duty to warn them. The court ruled that a jury might find that the family members were foreseeable victims of the woman's dangerous driving, and thus the psychiatrist may have had a duty to warn them.

It is worth noting that the *Schuster* court also held that the psychiatrist may be liable for failing to institute commitment proceedings because he had determined that the woman was a danger to the public. Counselors should always consider taking more generalized steps to protect the public, such as informing the police or instituting commitment proceedings, any time they consider warning third parties.

The *Schuster* case represents probably the broadest extension of the duty-to-warn doctrine. Counselors in all states that either reject the communicated threat requirement, or have no duty-to-warn statutes or case law (see the Duty-to-Warn Exception chapter), must consider the possibility of warning foreseeable victims of clients known to drive recklessly.

Criminals
Prison mental health professionals whose violent or sexual-criminal clients are about to be paroled must notify appropriate authorities or potential victims if these clients' propensities constitute a danger. In recent years, paroled sexual predators have been known to abduct and kill young girls.

Danger to Self

As confidential information may at times be disclosed when clients are found to be dangerous to others, so also may disclosure be appropriate when a client is a danger to him- or herself. Here disclosures are intended to protect the client's own life and safety. In order to understand the parameters of this exception to confidentiality, counselors must be aware of the legal and ethical duties they owe to their suicidal clients.

Counselors have an absolute duty, in most situations, both to predict the suicidal tendencies of their clients and to take steps to prevent impending self-destruction. There are three ways that counselors can violate this duty and thus become vulnerable to legal or professional sanctions:

1. **Assistance of suicide.** The first issue here is whether the counselor took any actions to assist the client's suicide, or intentionally ignored his or her duty to prevent it. The second issue is whether such actions or inactions were a direct cause of the suicide or suicidal attempt. Because assisting suicide is a crime, any actions in furtherance of a client's suicidal plans are likely to lead to criminal prosecution as well as civil liability. Directing a client to commit suicide, making suicidal instruments available to a client, mistreating a depressed or suicidal client, and encouraging the abuse of medication are among actions that may be considered suicidal assistance.

2. **Negligent diagnosis.** Any time a counselor fails to diagnose as suicidal a client who later commits suicide, he or she may be held liable for negligent diagnosis. Counselors may also be held liable for negligent diagnosis when an undiagnosed client unsuccessfully attempts suicide, resulting in physical and emotional injury to the client or to family members. Liability under negligent diagnosis is likely to arise when the diagnostic data used for the misdiagnosis should have led a reasonably prudent professional to arrive at the conclusion that the client was indeed suicidal. Schutz (1982) has listed several demographic, social, and psychological predisposing factors helpful in understanding and predicting suicide.

3. **Abandonment.** The mismanagement of a client diagnosed as suicidal by a counselor who was either unavailable or unresponsive to the client's emergency situation is seen as abandonment. When a client has been accurately diagnosed as suicidal, the failure of a counselor to properly manage and treat that client to aver suicide or its attempt may result in criminal and civil liability. Courts are likely to look at the what, how, when, and where of the counselor's behavior after it became obvious that a client was suicidal. When one set of professional choices of action seems clearly superior and could have prevented the client's suicide or attempt but the

counselor failed to choose that alternative, a presumption of abandonment or mismanagement may attach. The counselor then bears the burden of proving that despite the availability of those apparently superior preventive measures his or her treatment choice was justifiable. That is, the counselor must prove that he or she could not have disrupted the client's foreseeable plan to commit suicide.

4. **Adolescent Self-Injury (Cutting).** The research consensus is that individuals and adolescents who engage in self-harm, burn, bruise, and self-cutting are seeking to transform emotional pain into physical pain. This view also advances the notion that this transformation or refocusing is a coping strategy which makes it easier to understand and manage the emotional pain. If and when we work with clients who exhibit such behavior, should counselors consider it a level of "danger-to-self" that warrants breach of confidentiality? In the United Kingdom, Australia, Belgium and Norway, public self-cutting or self-injury are not classically considered suicidal attempts Moyer, M., & Nelson, K.W. (2007, October). Counselors should consider a number of issues in determining the danger posed and if it is reportable under the duty-to-warn exception.

   a. The age of the client. As a rule school counselors and those who work with children should not keep self-cutting confidential. They should consult with other professionals and/or with parents and effectively address the underlining reasons for the self-cutting.

   b. Children with compromised mental condition. Because self-cutting in this population can be deadly, confidentiality should bow to safety.

Evaluation of Suicidal Tendencies

Before any breach of confidentiality, the counselor should thoroughly evaluate the client's suicidal tendencies. In many cases, precise prediction of suicide is difficult. However, the process of evaluation must meet the *reasonable professional care* standard. Thus the counselor should evaluate the client's suicidal tendencies to the best of his or her ability as a mental health professional. The counselor should be able to demonstrate that other reasonable professionals under the same circumstances would have come to the same conclusion on whether the client was in fact suicidal.

The following guidelines are helpful in evaluation suicidal tendencies:

Cognitive-behavioral assessment
- Has this client attempted suicide before?
- Has this client ever assisted anyone in attempting suicide?
- Is the client thinking of suicide?
- Is the client engaged in farewell behavior to friends and relatives?
- Does the client usually behave impulsively?

Social and affective assessment
- Does the client feel lonely and isolated?
- Is the client giving away prized possessions?
- Has the client recently experienced a major loss of job, friend, family member, personal ability/quality?
- Is he or she in failing health or a failing marriage?
- Are dangerous instruments readily available to the client and does he/she plan to use them?
- Is the client depressed, anxious, or frustrated with life?
- Does the client have strong religious beliefs against suicide?

Who Should Be Warned

Once a client has been diagnosed as suicidal, who may ethically and legally be informed? The simple answer is that only those persons in a position, socially or professionally, to take responsibility or to play a role in helping the client should be warned or notified of the situation.

For example, it may be appropriate to notify the police, but it is never appropriate to notify the media. It may also be appropriate to notify parents or family members, but it might not be appropriate to notify a client's friends, unless such friends can provide real assistance in short-circuiting the client's suicidal plans. The professional litmus test as to who to inform is whether that individual has a social or professional obligation to do something about the client's situation. At this time, there is no case law holding a counselor liable for wrongfully disclosing a client's suicidal plan to individuals with no foreseeable role in averting the suicide. Such a case however, is foreseeable; and counselors must be careful to warn only those who need to be warned.

Content of Warning

How much of what a counselor knows about his or her suicidal client should be communicated to police, family members, friends, hospital personnel, crisis center professionals, or anyone else who can help avert an impending suicide? Does the fact that a client is suicidal justify wholesale disclosure of the entire contents of the client's file to potential helpers? Clearly it does not.

A determination that a significant suicidal risk exists justifies the disclosure only of that amount of information necessary to prevent the client from committing suicide. The fact that a client is suicidal, the methods or means the client has chosen to take his or her life, and the time and place of the expected act all might be appropriately revealed to a client's friends, the police, and crisis centers. More detailed mental health information, such as the client's diagnosis and any precipitating events, should only be revealed to professionals who are equipped to use that information to help avert the suicide.

It is unprofessional to reveal a client's personal information to individuals who cannot use that information in the best interest of the client. When a counselor reveals a client's private data simply because that client is suicidal, it constitutes a breach of confidentiality. Nevertheless, counselors have an ethical obligation not only to reveal only relevant information to appropriate persons but also to reveal *sufficient* information. A counselor could be held liable if he or she knew, but failed to supply, information that might have helped others save the life of the client.

The Involuntary Commitment Option

An option available to counselors with suicidal clients is the initiation of involuntary commitment proceedings. When a clear suicidal diagnosis cannot be made, but the evidence points in the direction of suicide, or when suicide has been diagnosed but no in-patient facility is immediately available to admit the client, the counselor may arrange for a brief (usually 72-hour) detention of the client. Most states have laws that permit such emergency custodial detention of any person reasonably believed to be disabled by a mental condition that poses a grave danger to self.

Such emergency involuntary commitment always requires an evaluation by designated state and mental health officials. If the evaluation confirms the counselor's suicidal concerns, the individual is admitted and treated in a hospital or in-patient clinic for 72 hours. If there is a positive change in mental status during this period, the client is released and referred for out-patient treatment. If the status remains the same or gets worse, the client may be detained for an additional period for more evaluation and treatment. Counselors are well advised to review and understand the commitment statute in the state in which they practice because of the potential for its abuse. The forms that such abuse may take depend upon the specific provisions of the statute. A local attorney should be consulted whenever there is doubt as to the legalities of a plan of action under a commitment law.

Death With Dignity

Most medical and mental health professional have traditionally and adamantly maintained that it is *always* unethical to facilitate the death of any person, even those who are terminally ill and have "rationally" decided to die with dignity. The only way to overcome this reluctance and resistance is for states to pass laws making it legal to facilitate death with dignity. Citizens of some states (California, for example) have tried unsuccessfully, to prosecute Dr. Kevorkian under existing criminal statutes. Not so long ago, the Michigan legislature passed a new law specifically prohibiting suicide assistance and in Baxter v Montana (2009) the Montana Supreme Court ruled that Montana constitution does not give a right for "aid in dying" or assisted suicide to its citizens.

Counselors should become familiar with their own state's law in this important area.

There have been very few court decisions dealing with suicide assistance issues. California appellate courts have held that a patient's constitutional right to privacy and autonomy (and by implication his or her right to choose to die with dignity) supersedes a physician's ethical duties. However, until the U.S. Supreme Court clearly speaks on the constitutionality of death with dignity, the matter will not be settled. Until then professionals who help their clients die could be inviting civil and criminal liability as well as professional sanctions. Death-with-dignity clients should be carefully evaluated and appropriate authorities and individuals notified. At this point in time, it is not professionally advisable for counselors to attempt to distinguish between *rational* and *irrational* suicidal plans in fulfilling their professional obligation to prevent suicide. Counselors should instead encourage their client to develop a living will or health care testament under the advisement of a lawyer. It is important to note that while a mental health professional may encourage their clients to consider developing a living will, the responsibility of making specific advisements regarding said will should be left to the client's legal advisor. The role the counselor should exclusively be to process the mental health aspects of having a terminal illness or developing a living will.

Frequently Asked Questions

Q. Your client tells you that 6 months ago he was involved in a bank robbery. He got $30,000 from the heist and is pleased that he was finally able to catch up with his bills and pay off his car loan. He believes that he needs counseling only for his compulsive spending behavior. You know that the police are still searching for the bank robbers. Do you have a duty to inform anyone?

A. Counselors should always be careful to distinguish their moral and civic duties from their ethical and legal duties. In this case, there is no ethical or legal obligation to inform the police, especially if the client does not plan to rob another bank. Even an anonymous call to the police will be unethical because the obligation to keep client disclosures confidential does not depend upon whether the breach might be discovered.

It is also important to note that the duty-to-warn exception applies only to *present and future dangers*, not to past ones, with the exception of past instances of child abuse or aged or disabled adult abuse (see the Danger to Others: Specific Groups chapter). Past dangerous behavior, of course, can and should be used to diagnose present and future dangerousness (see the Concept of Dangerousness chapter).

Q. You are a school counselor, and in compliance with your school's administrative guidelines, you informed the principal of your intention to notify the police of a serious homicidal threat made by a student. The principal is worried that bringing in the police might result in bad publicity for the school and urges you to reconsider. You believe that this child poses a real and imminent threat to the safety to others. What should you do?

A. This again may depend upon the specific statutes that apply in your state. Some states have statutes that only require a counselor to report the situation to a superior. The precise language of the reporting statute is important.

In states without such limiting statutes, if there is a specific threat directed at an identifiable person, you clearly have a duty to warn not only the police but also the intended victim. If the intended victim is not clear, you should seek legal advice before warning potential victims because you may be held liable to your client for breach of confidentiality and warning when not required. There may, of course, be additional unpleasant repercussions from disobeying the instructions of your principal. But your ultimate decision on whether or not to warn should be based on sound professional concerns rather than on administrative speculations or sympathies.

Q. Should a counselor inform all clients of the duty-to-warn exception to confidentiality before the establishment of the counselor-client relationship? If so, isn't there a risk that such disclosure may deter a dangerous client from discussing his or her violent urges with the counselor, thus interfering with successful counseling and posing a danger to the public?

A. A recent study found very little evidence that providing clients with information about confidentiality exceptions inhibited client disclosure (Muehleman, Pickens, & Robinson, 1985). Moreover, the concept of informed consent *requires* that clients be notified of all known or potential risks associated with the use of a counselor's services. Informed consent is intended to protect clients' privacy rights. And failure to provide full information on confidentiality and its exceptions is a breach of this requirement as well as a denial of a client's right to privacy. The result might be a suit for breach of confidentiality or violation of privacy if the counselor does warn intended victims. Realistically, the client probably will not prevail in court if the diagnosis accurately indicated that he or she did have dangerous propensities that required the counselor to warn potential victims; but professional ethics, and prudence, still mandate disclosure of confidentiality limits at the outset of the relationship.

Q. Can you be held liable for a violation of the duty to warn even if you are not certified or licensed?

A. Any mental health professional-counselor, social worker, psychologist, psychiatrist-can be held liable for failing to warn when required if there is a *genuine psychotherapist-client relationship* between that professional and the dangerous client. The duty is predicated on the counseling relationship and not on certification or licensure.

Q. Your client has a history of dangerous acting out. He recently lost his job, has become more depressed, and may be ready to explode. You plan to take a month-long vacation out of town. Do you have a duty to inform anyone?

A. Not necessarily. There is some diagnostic uncertainty as to whether this client is imminently dangerous. However, before going on such a long vacation, it is consistent with the spirit of the duty-to-warn rule to institute a prudent management program for this client. Referral to an interim professional and a contract with the client to check into a hospital if his or her condition worsens seems appropriate under the circumstances. Failure to institute such a program could be considered tantamount to abandonment and mismanagement (see the Danger to Self chapter).

Q. Your client tells you he is HIV positive, does not intend to tell his girl friend of his status, and does plan to continue to have unsafe sex with her. Do you have an obligation to warn her?

A. There clearly appears to be a duty to warn, even in those states that have adopted the narrowest duty-to-warn requirements, because there is a specific, communicated threat to an easily identifiable individual (see the Duty-to-Warn Exception and Danger to Others: Specific Groups chapters). The risk of serious bodily harm is undisputed because HIV is transmitted through unprotected sexual contact, the ultimate result of HIV infection is death, and there is currently no cure for AIDS.

Counselors do, however, have an ethical obligation, before warning anyone, to first utilize appropriate counseling or other psychosocial interventions to try to prevent the danger. One possible approach is to explain the danger inherent in the intended conduct (which could include criminal liability in some states) and attempt to induce the client to reconsider. Another is to ask the client to inform his intended "victim" of his HIV status. Only when all such interventions have failed should the sex partner be warned.

One factor that should be considered is whether the identifiable sex partner and the HIV-positive client have already been sexually intimate for an extended period. If so, HIV most likely has already been transmitted. However, even in such cases a warning (if allowed by state law) still seems appropriate because it may enable the sex partner to get adequate evaluation and treatment. It is hoped that he or she will then become a responsible sex partner should he or she choose to remain sexually active. Overall, the best approach is clearly to warn the partner, on the assumption that he or she is not yet infected. But the counselor must be absolutely sure of the facts before giving out such information, given state statutes that specifically prohibit the release of information on HIV status under most circumstances.

Q. Your client is 87 years old. After many car accidents caused by poor and inattentive driving, his license was revoked, and he must not depend upon rides to get to appointments. Last Monday he drove himself because he could not get a ride. He reported being very nervous as he drove but promised to be very careful while driving home. You informed him of the duty-to-warn exception before he began counseling 2 years ago. He did drive home safely as promised, but you wonder whether you should have notified the police or taken other steps to ensure the safety of local pedestrians and drivers.

A. Because of this client's past driving record and present anxiety, there appears to have been a real danger of another accident. You might have incurred liability to accident victims because you took no steps to protect them by notifying local police. In states that require specifically communicated threats to readily identified victims, the duty to warn probably ends there; but in states like

Wisconsin you might also be required to warn likely passengers. This once again points up the necessity for all mental health professionals to familiarize themselves with the parameters of the duty-to-warn rule in their own states.

Case Law Digests

Selected List of Related Cases:
- *Boyton v. Burglass*
  590 So.2d 446 (1991).
- *Brooks v. Logan*
  130 Idaho574 (1997).
- *Brown v. Smith*
  Conn Super.LEXIS 2227 (2001).
- *Emerich v. Philadelphia Center for Human Development, Inc.* 554 Pa. 209,
  720 A.2d 1032 (1998).
- *Green v. Ross*
  691 So.2d.542 (1997).
- *Hamman v. County of Maricopa*
  161 Ariz. 58, 775 P.2d 1122 (1989).
- *Hesler v. Osawatowie State Hospital*
  266 Kan. 616 (1999).
- *Jablonski v. United States*
  712 F.2d 391 (1983)
- *Lipari v. Sears Roebuck & Co*
  497 F.Supp. 185 (D. Neb. 1980).
- *McIntosh v. Milano*
  168 N.J. Super. 466, 403 A2d 500 (1979).
- *Sheron v. Lutheran Medical Center*
  18 P.3d 796 (2000).
- *Tarasoff v. Regents of the University of California*
  17 Cal.3d 425 (1976).
- *Thapar v Zezulka*
  994 S.W. 2d 635 (1999).
- *Thompson v. County of Alameda*
  27 Cal.3d 741, 614 P2d. 728, 167 Cal Rptr. 70 (1980).

Summary of Cases

Tarasoff is the flagship case and sets the overarching standard for duty-to-warn cases. It makes it mandatory as a matter of law for mental health practitioners to breach content and contact confidentiality by notifying a potential third party victim or others whenever a client's specific promises and propensities will foreseeably harm others. Not only has this been broadly adopted in many jurisdictions, it has been infused into the professional and ethical standards of all mental health professions.

In *Jablonski*, a federal court concluded that the *Tarasoff* specific-threat-made-to-a-specific-third-party standard includes when a victim is "sufficiently targeted." This means that mental health practitioners must look at the totality of the circumstances to determine who may be victimized not just the verbal threats made against a specific person. This broadens the standard from specific to reasonably foreseeable victim. This means that the duty may be owed to whoever is in foreseeable danger of being harmed by the client. The public at large or classes of people may be viewed as foreseeable victim under *Jablonski*. If this is the case, the mental health practitioner, now has a duty not to notify all potential victims, as this may be impossible, but rather to detain or involuntarily hospitalize the client.

Many states that have adopted *Tarasoff*, have not adopted the broad version expressed in *Jablonski*. They instead favor the *specific-threat-specific-victim* version. It is therefore unlikely these jurisdictions will be in any hurry to consider principles discussed earlier.

Texas courts remain the most conservative, choosing not to create the *Tarrasoff* duty. In *Thapar*, the Supreme Court of Texas, interpreting Tex.Gen.Laws 512, specifically asserted that the only exception in Texas Confidentiality Statute is the provision that permits disclosure to law enforcement personnel. Under this law, Dr. Thapas was permitted to disclose the danger to law enforcement but not required (had no duty) to notify the potential victim.

Guidelines for Practice

To fulfill all ethical and legal duties to protect your client and others from potential harm while safeguarding client privacy to the fullest extent possible

1. Fully disclose your legal responsibilities to breach confidentiality in duty-to-warn situations at the outset of counseling.
2. Purchase professional liability insurance. In the event that your decision to warn, or not to warn, results in harm to your client or another person, you will need an attorney to represent you.
3. Be absolutely clear, before a duty-to-warn situation arises, what the duty-to-warn rule is in your state.

In those states with statutory or case law to guide you (about half the states) . . .

1. Find out if a communicated threat is necessary to trigger a duty to warn.
2. Find out if the intended victim must be clearly identified or only reasonably identifiable.
3. Remember these are important issues because you may be held liable either for failing to warn those entitled to a warning, or for warning those not so entitled.
4. Discuss the meaning of your state's law with your supervisor, other professionals, or an attorney if some or all aspects are not clear to you.

In those states with no legal precedent . . .

1. Look to the ethical guidelines for your profession. These are helpful in determining when local authorities may be informed about a dangerous client, although they offer little real help in deciding whether or not to warn specific private individuals.
2. Refer to the Concept of Dangerousness chapter for assistance.
   Discuss the matter with a supervisor, other professionals, or a local attorney before warning private individuals. There may not be a settled statutory or case law covering the duty-to-warn situation, but there may be a commonly accepted rule that is generally followed in your jurisdiction.
3. Warn only those who are truly in danger. That is, warn the person or persons when the client clearly communicates a threat of physical harm and specifically directs that threat.
4. Use your professional judgment when the threat is not specific and the intended victim not clear.

If a client makes an explicit threat . . .

1. Attempt to dissuade the client from following through with the threat.
2. Suggest that he or she check into a hospital if this seems appropriate.
3. Perhaps attempt to induce the client to contract with you not to carry out the threat.

If the client agrees to a contract not to carry out a threat . . .

1. Use your professional judgment in deciding whether the client seems sincere in withdrawing the threat or whether the danger to others still exists.
2. Consider whether this client has kept his or her word with respect to other contracts you have made in the past.

If you are still convinced that others may be in danger . . .
1. Discuss the matter with your client and inform him or her of your legal responsibility to warn others.
2. *However:* Before revealing your intention to warn third parties, assess the situation fully. It is conceivable that a violent and angry client might be induced to follow through with his or her threat, or might act out in some other way, if informed of your intention to warn others.
3. Discuss the potentially dangerous situation and your intention to warn others with a supervisor or another professional.
4. Contact the police and inform them of the situation. Be careful to disclose only as much information as actually needed to address the danger.
5. Notify the intended victim. Limit disclosure to what is necessary for that person's protection.
6. Consider taking steps to have the client involuntarily committed to a psychiatric hospital pursuant to state law.

Summary

Mental health professional have a general ethical and legal obligation not to disclose client confidences. It is important for all professionals to become familiar with applicable codes of ethics and state privilege laws.

At the outset of counseling, clients should be made fully aware of the meaning of confidentiality and the exceptions to it that may apply. Confidentiality may be waived, but the waiver must be knowing and voluntary. The special needs of minors and incompetents with respect to the waiver of confidentiality must be understood by all counselors.

One important exception to confidentiality occurs when a client poses an imminent threat of harm to self or others. In such cases, the counselor may have a duty to breach confidentiality for the protection of the client and the community. Counselors must learn the parameters of the duty-to-warn exception in the state in which they practice for their own protection and for the protection of their clients and society.

Discussion Questions

1. Under what specific circumstances in your state does a mental health professional have a duty to warn?

2. What are the legal and ethical justifications for the duty-to-warn exception? What professional reservations, if any, do you have about this rule?

3. What circumstances must be present in order to trigger a duty to warn third parties? What professional obligations does a counselor owe his or her client before acting on the duty-to-warn exception?

4. Which cases discussed in this book do you consider most important relative to the duty-to-warn exception? If these cases did not originate in your state, have your state's courts followed the rulings in those cases? Which case in your state is most important with respect to the duty-to-warn exception?

5. Dangerousness is a prerequisite for the exercise of the duty-to-warn exception. How will you go about predicting dangerousness to others? What issues make the prediction of dangerousness difficult?

6. Involuntary commitment is one option for mental health professionals who are faced with a dangerous client. Under what circumstances might you use it, and for what purposes?

7. Child, elder, and disabled abuse protection laws require counselors and other mental health professionals to report incidents of abuse to appropriate state agencies. If you find out that your 11-year-old client was sexually abused by a family member 2 years ago, do you have a duty to report the abuse? Might your answer be different if the incident occurred 3 months ago?

8. Your client walks into your office for his fourth session and says, "The result is finally in. I am indeed HIV positive, but I have been assured that this does not mean that I will develop full-blown AIDS. I therefore have decided to go ahead and marry Susan as planned. I don't think it's necessary to inform her of my HIV status until after we are marries, as this may alarm her unnecessarily." Do you as a counselor have a duty to warn Susan? Justify your answer ethically and legally.

46   Discussion Questions

9. How might you handle a client who tells you of his plan to die with dignity as a result of his HIV infection? How might you react if he has chosen the time and place and asked for your cooperation?

10. Your client tells you of his plan to set his girl friend's car on fire because she is cheating on him. He plans to do it in a way that ensures that no one will be hurt. Do you have a duty to warn her, or law enforcement officials? Suppose, instead, he told you that he will encourage his friends to steal her car. He is certain this will hurt her emotionally. How might you react professionally? Do you have a duty to warn her?

11. Do you believe that the concept of informed consent requires counselors to notify clients of the duty-to-warn exception to confidentiality? What if you are concerned that your client may harm his intended victim immediately if you tell him of your intention to warn her?

12. Do you as a mental health professional see any difference between situations requiring mandatory as opposed to discretionary reporting of confidential client information? Can you think of a situation in which reporting should be mandatory? Can you change the facts so that it becomes a discretionary reporting situation?

13. What do you think are the pitfalls of e-communication of dangerousness to others? Which e-communication method will you use if your client will foreseeably harm his former girlfriend Linda who is on her way back from vacation in England with her new boyfriend Fred?

Suggested Readings

Because duty-to-warn law is so complex and diverse, we have included an extensive list of suggested readings for those professionals who are eager to learn more.

Ahia, C. E. (2009). *Legal and Ethical Dictionary for Mental Health Professionals 2nd Edition.* Lanham, MD: University Press of America Inc.

Anderson, J. R., & Barret, B. (Eds.). (2001). *Ethics in HIV-related psychotherapy: Clinical decision making in complex cases.* Washington, DC: American Psychological Association.

Appelbaum, P.S. (1985). *Tarasoff* and the clinician: Problems in fulfilling the duty to protect. *American Journal of Psychiatry, 142*(4), 425-429

Arthur, G.L., Jr., & Swanson, C.D. (1993). *Confidentiality and privileged communication* (ACA Legal Series, Vol. 6). Alexandria, VA: American Counseling Association.

Atkins, C. (2007). My patient is moving to another state . . . Can I continue therapy over the phone and/or Internet? *The Therapist, 19*(2), 16-18

Barnett, J. E. (1999b). Recordkeeping: Clinical, ethical and risk management issues. In L. VandeCreek & T. Jackson (Eds.), *Innovations in clinical practice: A source book* (vol. 17, pp. 237-254). Sarasota, FL: Professional Resource Press.

Barnett, J. E., & Johnson, W. B. (2010). *Ethics desk reference for counselors.* Alexandria, VA: American Counseling Association.

Barnett, J.E., MacGlashan, S. G., & Clarke, A. J. (2000). Risk management and ethical issues regarding termination and abandonment, In L. VandeCreek & T. Jackson (Eds.). *Innovations in clinical practice: A source book* (vol. 18, pp. 231-246). Sarasota, FL: Professional Resource Press.

Barnett, J. E. & Porter, J. E. (1998). The suicidal patient: Clinical and risk management strategies. In L. VandeCreek, S. Knapp, & T. Jackson (Eds.), *Innovations in clinical practice: A source book* (vol.16, pp. 95-107). Sarasota, FL: Professional Resource Press.

Barnett, J. E., Wise, E. H., Johnson-Greene, D., & Bucky, S. F. (2007). Informed consent: Too much of a good thing or not enough? *Professional Psychology: Research and Practice, 38*(2), 179-186

Bednar, R. L., Bednar, S. C., Lambert, M. J., & Waite, D. R. (1991). *Psychotherapy with high-risk clients: Legal and professional standards.* Belmont, CA: Brooks/Cole, Cengage Learning.

Benitez, B. R. (2004). Confidentiality, and its exceptions, *The Therapist, 16*(4), 32036.

Bennett, A. G., & Werth, J. L., Jr. (2006). Working with clients who may harm themselves, In B. Herlihy & G. Corey (Eds.), *ACA ethical standards casebook* (6ᵗʰ ed., pp. 223-228). Alexandria, VA: American Counseling Association.

Bennett, B. E., Bricklin, P. M., Harris, E., Knapp, S., vandeCreek, L., & Younggren, J. N. (2006). *Assessing and managing risk in psychological practice: An individualize approach.* Rockville, MD: The Trust.

Bennett, B. E., Bryant, B. K., VandenBos, G. R., & Greenwood, A. (1990). *Professional liability and risk management.* Washington, DC: American Psychological Association

Berman, A.L., & Cohen-Sandler, R. (1983). Suicide and mal-practice expert testimony and the standard of care. *Professional Psychology: Research and Practice, 4*(1), 6-19

Bersoff, D.N. (1976). Therapists as protectors and policemen: New roles as a result of *Tarasoff. Professional Psychology, 6,* 267-273

Best, R. (2006, May). Deliberate self-harm: A challenge for schools. *British Journal of Guidance & Counseling 34*(2), 161-175. doi: 10.1080/03069880600583196

Burns, R.E. (1975). Psychotherapist-patient privilege, patients' dangerous condition in confidentiality, legal duty to warn potential victim. *Akron Law Review, 9*(1), 191-198

Bursten, B. (1978). Dimensions of third-party protection. *Bulletin of the American Academy of Law and Psychiatry, 6*(4), 405-413

Cassidy, P.S. (1974). The liability of psychiatrists for malpractice. *University of Pittsburgh Law Review, 36,* 108-137.

Cohen, E.D. (1990). Confidentiality, counseling, and clients who have AIDS: Ethical foundations of a model rule. *Journal of Counseling and Development, 68*(3), 282-286

Daley, D.W. (1975). *Tarasoff* and the psychotherapist's duty to warn. *San Diego Law Review, 12,* 932-956

Dimmock, M., Grieves, S., & Place, M. (2008). Young people who cut themselves – a growing challenge for educational settings. *British Journal of Special Education, 35*(1), 42-48

Dix, G.E. (1981). *Tarasoff* and the duty to warn potential victims. In C.K. Hofling (Ed.), *Law and ethics in the practice of psychiatry.* New York: Brunner/Mazel.

Everstine, L., Everstine, D.S., Heymann, G.M., True, R.H., Frey, D.H., Johnson, H.G., & Seiden, R.H. (1980). Privacy and confidentiality in psychotherapy. *American Psychologist, 35*(9) 828-840

Froeschle, J., & Moyer, M. (2004, April). Just cut it out: Legal and ethical changes in counseling students who self-mutilate. *Professional School Counseling, 7*(4), 231-235.

Glassman, M.S. (1975). Confidential communications-privileged communications, psychiatry-psychotherapist has a duty to warn an endangered victim who peril was disclosed by communications between the psychotherapist and patient. *Cincinnati Law Review, 44,* 368-375

Griffith, E.J., & Griffith, E.E.H. (1978). Duty to third parties dangerousness, and the right to refuse treatment: Problematic concepts for psychiatrist and lawyer. *California Western Law Review, 14*(2), 241-274

Grossman, M. (1978). Right to privacy vs. right to know. In W.E. Barton & C.J. Sanborn (Eds.), *Law and the mental health professions: Friction at the interface.* New York: International Universities Press.

Gurevitch, H. (1977). *Tarasoff:* Protective privilege versus public peril. *American Journal of Psychiatry, 134,* 289-292

Hawton, K., & Harriss, L. (2007, Spring). Deliberate self-harm by under 15-year-olds: characteristics, trends, and outcome. *The Journal of Child Psychology and Psychiatry, 49*(4), 441-448. doi:10.1111/j.1469-7610.2007.01852.x

Henderson, D. (1987). Negligent liability and the foreseeability factor. *Journal of Counseling and Development, 66*(2), 86-89.

Herlihy, B., & Sheeley, V. (1988). Counselor liability and the duty to warn. Selected cases, statutory trends, and implications for practice. *Counselor Education and Supervision, 27*(3), 203-215.

Howell, J.A. (1978). Civil liability for suicide: An analysis of the causation issue. *Arizona State Law Journal,* pp. 578-615.

Jacobson, C.M., Muehlenkamp, J.J., Miller, A. L., & Turner, J. B. (2008). Psychiatric impairment among adolescents engaging in different types of deliberate self-harm. *Journal of Clinical Child & Adolescent Psychology, 37*(2), 363-375.

Kermani, E.J., & Drob, S.L. (1987). *Tarasoff* decision: A decade later dilemma still faces psychotherapist. *American Journal of Psychotherapy, 41*(2), 271-285

Lee, J.V. (1977). A psychotherapist who knows or should know his patient intends violence to another incurs a duty to warn. *Cumberland Law Review, 7,* 550-559

Lee, V. (1976). The dangerous patient exception and the duty to warn: Creation of a dangerous precedent. *University of California, Davis Law Review, 9,* 549-568.

Leonard, J.B. (1977). A therapist's duty to potential victims: A nonthreatening view of *Tarasoff. Law and Human Behavior, 1,* 309-317

Madge, N., Hewitt, A., Hawton, K., Jan de Wilde, E., Corcoran, P., Fekete, S., De Leo, D. (2008, November). Deliberate self-harm within an international community sample of young people: comparative findings from the child & adolescent self-harm in Europe study. *The Journal of Child Psychology and Psychiatry, 49*(6) 667-677

Malcolm, J.J. (1975). Duty imposed upon psychotherapists to exercise reasonable care to warn potential victims of foreseeably imminent dangers posed by mentally ill patients. *Seton Hall Law Review, 6,* 536-550

Megargee, E.J. (1970). The prediction of violence with psychological tests. In C. Spelberger (Ed.) *Current topics in clinical and community psychology.* New York: Academic Press.

Miller, D.J., & Thelen, M.H. (1987). Confidentiality in psychotherapy: History, issues, and research. *Psychotherapy, 24*(4), 704-711

Monahan, J. (1981). The prediction of violent behavior: Developments in psychology and law. In C.J. Scheirer & B.L. Hammonds (Eds.), *Psychology and the law* (pp. 147-176). Washington, DC: American Psychological Association.

Morrow, K. (1976). Psychotherapist has a duty to warn an endangered victim whose peril was disclosed to psychotherapists by patient. *North Dakota Law Review, 53,* 179-284

Moyer, M., & Nelson, K. W. (2007, October). Investigating and understanding self-mutilation: The student voice. *Professional School Counseling, 11*(1), 42-48

Olander, A.J. (1978). Discovery of psychotherapist-patient communications after *Tarasoff. Sand Diego Law Review, 15,* 265-285.

Oldham, J.T. (1987). Liability of therapists to nonpatients. *Journal of Clinical Child Psychology, 3,* 187-188.

Olsen, T.A. (1977). Imposing a duty to warn on psychiatrists: A judicial threat to the psychiatric profession. *University of Colorado Law Review, 48,* 283-310

Paul, R.E. (1977). *Tarasoff* and the duty to warn: Toward a standard of conduct that balances the rights of clients against the rights of third parties. *Professional Psychology, 7,* 125-128.

Pendley, W.P. (1977). The dangerous psychiatric patient: The doctor's duty to warn. *Land and Water Law Review, 10,* 593-606.

Perr, I.N. (1960). Suicide responsibilities of hospital and psychiatrist. *Cleveland-Marshall Law Review, 3*(9), 427-440.

Pietrofesa, J.J., Pietrofesa, C.J., & Pietrofesa, J.D. (1990). The mental health counselor and "duty to warn." *Journal of Mental Health Counseling, 12*(2), 129-137

Pope, K.S. (1985). The suicidal client: Guidelines for assessment and treatment. *California State Psychologist,* July-August, pp.1-2

Rachlin, S., & Schwartz, H.I. (1986). Unforeseeable liability for patients' violent acts. *Hospital and Community Psychiatry, 37*(7), 725-731

Remley, T. P. (2004). Suicide and the law. In D. Capuzzi (Ed.), *Suicide across the life span: Implications for counselors* (pp. 185-210). Alexandria, VA: American Counseling Association.

Remley, T. P. (2009). Legal challenges in counseling suicidal students. In D. Capuzzi, *Suicide prevention in the schools: Guidelines for middle and high school settings* (2nd ed., pp. 71-83). Alexandria, VA: American Counseling Association.

Remley, T. P., & Herlihy, B. (2010). *Ethical, legal, and professional issues in counseling* (3rd ed.). Upper Saddle River, NJ: Merrill/Prentice Hall.

Roth, L.H., & Meisel, A. (1977). Dangerousness, confidentiality, and the duty to warn. *American Journal of Psychiatry, 134,* 508-511

Rozovsky, F.A. (1984). *Consent to treatment: A practical guide.* Boston: Little, Brown.

Ruthledge, C. M., Rimer, D., & Scott, M. (2008, September). Vulnerable goth teens: The role of schools in this psychosocial high-risk culture. *Journal of School Health, 78*(9), 459-464.

Schutz, B.M. (1982). *Legal liability in psychotherapy.* San Franciso: Jossey-Bass.

Schwartz, V.E. (1971). Civil liability for causing suicide: A synthesis of law and psychiatry. *Vanderbilt Law Review, 24,* 217-256

Selekman, M. D. (2010, January). Helping self-harming students. *Educational Leadership,* 48-53.

Sim, L., Adrian, M., Zeman, J., Cassano, M., & Friedrich, W. N. (2009). Adolescent deliberate self-harm: Linkages to emotion regulation and family emotional climate. *Journal of Research on Adolescence, 19*(1), 75-91

Simm, R., Roen, K., & Daiches, A. (2008, April). Educational professionals' experiences of self-harm in primary school children: 'You don't really believe, unless you see it'. *Oxford Review of Education, 34*(2), 253-269. doi: 10.1080/03054980701663967

Simpson, C. (2001). Self-mutilation. *ERIC/CASS Digest,* 1-6.

Slovenko, R. (1973). *Psychiatry and law.* Boston: Little, Brown.

Stadler, H.A. (1986). *Confidentiality: The professional's dilemma: Participant manual.* Alexandria, VA: American Association for Counseling and Development.

Stone, A.A. (1976). The *Tarasoff* decision: Suing psychotherapists to safeguard society. *Harvard Law Review, 90,* 358-378

Szasz, T. (1986). The case against suicide prevention. *American Psychology, 41*(7), 806-812.

Tabachnick, N.D., & Farberow, N.L. (1961). The assessment of self-destructive potentiality. In N.L. Farberow & E.S. Schneid-man (Eds.), *The cry for help.* New York: McGraw-Hill.

Teufel, J.A., Brown, S. L., & Birch, D.A. (2007, Spring). Reports of self-harm and social stressors among early adolescents: A brief report. *The Health Educator, 39*(1), 18-23

Vandercreek, L., & Knapp, S. (1984). Counselors, confidentiality, and life-endangering clients. *Counselor Education and Supervision, 24*(1), 51-57.

Vandercreek, L., Knapp, S., & Herzog, C. (1987). Malpractice risks in the treatment of dangerous patients. *Psychotherapy, 24*(2), 145-153.

Waldo, S. L., & Malley, P. (1992). *Tarasoff* and its progeny: Implications for the school counselor. *The School Counselor, 40,* 46-54

Welfel, E. R. (2009). Emerging issues in the duty to protect, In J. L. Werth Jr., E. R. Welfel, & G. A. H. Benjamin, (Eds.), *The duty to protect: Ethical, legal and professional considerations for mental health professionals* (pp. 229-248). Washinton, DC: American Psychological Association.

Welfel, E. R., Werth, J. L., Jr., & Benjamin, G. A. H. (2009). Introduction to the duty to protect. In. J. L. Werth Jr., E. R. Welfel, & G. A. H. Benjamin (Eds.), *The duty to protect: Ethical, legal, and professional considerations for mental health professionals* (pp. 3-8). Washington, DC: American Psychological Association.

Wenk, E., Ribison, J., & Smith, G. (1972). Can violence be predicted? *Crime and Delinquency, 18,* 393.

Werth, J. L., Jr., & Belvins, D. (Eds.). (2006). *Psychosocial issues near the end of life. A resource for professional care providers.* Washinton, DC: American Psychological Association

Werth, J. L., & Crow, L. (2009). End-of-life care: An overview for professional counselors. *Journals of Counseling and Development, 87*(2), 194-202.

Werth, J. L., Jr., & Holdwick, D. J. (2000). A primer on rational suicide and other forms of hastened death. *The Counseling Psychologist, 28*(4), 511-539

Werth, J. L., Jr., & Kleespies, P. M. (2006). Ethical considerations in providing psychological services in end-of-life-care. In J. L. Werth Jr. & D. Blevins (Eds.), *Psychosocial issues near the end of life: A resource for professional care providers* (pp. 57-87). Washinton, DC: American Psychological Association.

Werth, J. L., Jr, & Richmond, J. (2009). End-of-life decisions and the duty to protect, In J. L. Werth Jr., E. R. Welfel, & G. A. H. Benjamin (Eds.), *The duty to protect: Ethical, legal, and professional considerations for mental health professionals* (pp. 195-208). Washinton, DC: American Psychological Association.

Werth, J. L., Jr., & Rogers J. R. (2005). Assessing for impaired judgment as a means of meeting the "duty to protect" when a client is a potential harm-to-self: Implications for clients making end-of-life decisions. *Mortality, 10,* 7-21

Werth, J. L. Jr., Welfel, E. R., & Benjamin, G. A. H. (Eds.). (2009). *The duty to protect: Ethical, legal, and professional considerations for mental health professionals.* Washington, DC: American Psychological Association.

Werth, J. L. Jr., Welfel, E. R., Benjamin, G. A. H., & Sales, B. D. (Eds.). (2009). Practice and policy responses to the duty to protect. In. J. L. Werth Jr., E. R. Welfel, & G. A. H. Benjamin (Eds.), *The duty to protect: Ethical, legal, and professional considerations for mental health professionals* (pp. 249-261). Washington, DC: American Psychological Association.

Wexler, D.B. (1979). Patients, therapists, and third parties: The victimological virtues of *Tarasoff. International Journal of Law and Psychiatry, 2,* 1-28.

Wineburgh, M. (1998). Ethics, managed cared, and outpatient psychotherapy. *Clinical Social Work Journal, 26*(4), 433-443.

Woody, R.H. (Ed.). (1984). *The law and the practice of human services.* San Francisco: Jossey-Bass

Woody, R.H. (1988). *Protecting your mental health practice.* San Francisco: Jossey-Bass.

Younggren, J. N., & Gottlieb, M. C. (2004). Managing risk when contemplating multiple relationships. *Professional Psychology: Research and Practice, 39*(5), 498-504

Zur, O. (2005). Tarasoff *statute in California: An update.* Retrieved February 1, 2005, from http://www.drzur.com/tarasoff.html

References

Ahia, C. E. (2009). *Legal and Ethical Dictionary for Mental Health Professionals 2ⁿᵈ Edition.* Lanham, MD: University Press of America Inc.

American Association for Counseling and Development. (1988). *Ethical standards.* Alexandria, VA: Author.

American Association for Counseling and Development. (1991). Report of the AACD Ethics Committee: 1989-1991. *Journal of Counseling and Development, 70*(2), 278-280.

American Association for Marriage and Family Therapy. (1991). *Code of ethics.* Washington, DC: Author.

American Mental Health Counselors Association. (1987). *Code of ethics for mental health counselors.* Alexandria, VA: Author

American Psychological Association. (1990). Ethical principles of psychologists (amended June 2, 1989). *American Psychologist, 45,* 390-395

American School Counselor Association. (1984). *Ethical standards for school counselors,* Falls Church, VA: Author.

Association for Specialists in Group Work. (1989). *Ethical guidelines for group counselors.* Alexandria, VA: Author.

Barry v. Turek, 267 Cal. Rptr (1990).

Cocozza & Steadman, (1975-1976). The failure of psychiatric predictions of dangerousness: Clear and convincing evidence. *Rutgers Law Review, 29,* 1084.

Herlihy, B., & Sheeley, V. (1987). Privileged communication in selected helping professions: A comparison among statutes. *Journal of Counseling and Development, 65*(9), 479-483.

Muehleman, T., Pickens, B., & Robinson, F. (1985). Informing clients about the limits to confidentiality, risks, and their rights: Is self-disclosure inhibited? *Professional Psychology Research and Practice, 16*(3), 385-397.

National Association of Alcoholism and Drug Abuse Counselors. (1987). *Ethical standards of alcoholism and drug abuse counselors.* Arlington, VA: Author

National Association of Social Workers. (1979). *Code of ethics.* Silver Spring, MD: Author.

Schuster v. Altenberg, 424 N.W 2d159 (1988).

Schutz, B.M. (1982). *Legal liability in psychotherapy.* San Francisco: Jossey-Bass

Shaw v. Glickman, 415A 2d 625 (Md. 1980).

Tarasoff v. Regents of the University of California, 131 Cal. Rptr (1976).

Thompson v. County of Alameda, 167 Cal. Rptr 70 (1980).

Each of the following has applicable statutes of interest to counselors in those states:

Colorado Revised Statutes (1987).

General Laws of Rhode Island (1987).

Kentucky Revised Statutes (1991).

Massachusetts General Laws Annotated (1992).

Minnesota Statutes Annotated (1989).

Montana Codes Annotated (1991).

New Hampshire Revised Statutes (1991).

New Jersey Statutes Annotated (1987).

Oklahoma Statutes Annotated (1992 Cumulative Pocket Part).

Oregon Revised Statutes (1985).

West's Annotated California Civil Code (1992 Cumulative Pocket Part).

West's Louisiana Statutes (1992).

Glossary

Civil Liability: When one person has damaged another by failing to fulfill an obligation to that person. Civil liability may arise as a result of intentional or unintentional (negligent) action or inaction.

Competence: In the therapeutic context, a client's ability to make proper life choices. A client who is unable to care for him- or herself may be declared legally incompetent and a guardian may be appointed to make decisions for him or her.

Confidentiality: The legal and ethical duty of counselors and other mental health professionals not to reveal information about their clients to unauthorized individuals. *Content confidentiality* requires that the substance of client-counselor discussions not be revealed; *contact confidentiality* requires that counselors not reveal the fact that a client is seeing a counselor. Because most laws do not protect contact confidentiality, separate contracts between individual clients and counselors may be required.

Criminal Liability: When a person's behavior violates specific criminal codes. Action against the violator is brought by the state. Violation of criminal codes may also lead to civil liability.

Dangerousness: In the context of counselor-client confidentiality, the likelihood that *physical harm* will occur to self or others as a result of a client's mental condition. Neither behavior that may cause emotional distress to self or others nor behavior that may potentially harm property is generally considered dangerous enough to warrant a breach of confidentiality. However, such dangerousness may be reportable if required by a specific state law.

Duty to Warn: A legal obligation of mental health professional to breach confidentiality and warn others when, by the standard of their profession, they determine that a client is a danger to self or others. Professionals are advised to look at the specific language of the statute or case law in their state to determine under what circumstances this duty may arise.

HIV-Specific Warning Legislation: Public health laws that specify the circumstances under which case4s of HIV infection may be reported. Counselors are advised to look carefully at such laws, which all states have, before making any such reports. In most states, only physicians have a duty to report HIV cases, although discretionary reporting may be made by others.

Informed Consent: A legal doctrine requiring physicians and mental health professionals to disclose adequately to clients the risks, advantages, and alternatives of proposed treatment. The doctrine presumes client competence and maturity as a guarantee that disclosure is understood. For minors and incompetents, the consent of a guardian may be substituted.

Voluntary and Involuntary Commitment: The dangerous mental condition of a client may justify holding him or her in a hospital or other facility to ensure that no serious harm is done to the client or others. Without the client's approval, this is called *involuntary commitment. Voluntary commitment* occurs when a client, acting either on his or her own volition or as a result of social or professional advice, checks into a facility for the purpose of mental treatment and evaluation in order to avoid the danger of mental deterioration.

About the Author

C. Emmanuel Ahia is a professor of counseling as well as the director of the Educational Specialist program at Rider University Graduate School, Lawrenceville, New Jersey. Dr. Ahia was formerly a counselor at the Center for Counseling and Psychological Services, University of Arkansas, Fayetteville, and special services counseling coordinator at Southern Illinois University, Carbondale. He was a past president of the New Jersey Association for Multicultural Counseling as well as Chair of the Ethics Board for the New Jersey Counselor Association. Dr. Ahia holds an MA from Wheaton College Graduate School, Illinois, a PhD in educational psychology (counseling) from Southern Illinois University, Carbondale, and a JD in law from the University of Arkansas, Fayetteville. He practices and consults with attorneys in the area of Mental Health Law. He has also taught mental health ethics and law courses at Central Michigan and John Hopkins Universities.